MOVING UP

Published in the UK by Scholastic, 2024
1 London Bridge, London, SE1 9BG
Scholastic Ireland, 89E Lagan Road, Dublin Industrial Estate, Glasnevin,
Dublin, D11 HP5F

ISBN 978 0702 33374 3

A CIP catalogue record for this book is available from the British Library.

Printed and bound in the UK by CPI Group (UK) Ltd, Croydon, CR0 4YY
Paper made from wood grown in sustainable forests and other controlled sources.

1 3 5 7 9 10 8 6 4 2

www.scholastic.co.uk

CHRISTIAN FOLEY

MOVING UP

How to Ace Secondary School

SCHOLASTIC

CONTENTS

INTRODUCTION

Here you are at the brink of a new beginning. Secondary school. Whether you're a fizzing firework of excitement and hope, feeling the nagging pinches of nerves, or all of those feelings at once, these words are for you. It's going to be fine.

BETTER than fine.

In this book we'll breakdown everything you might be worrying about and help you look forward to what's to come. Right now, your secondary school days are a blank canvas, about to be painted by a wonderful mix of exciting new experiences. You're going to learn about incredible stuff, meet brilliant people and create a world of opportunities for your bright future.

Things are changing. You're making the famous move from being the big bosses on the benches, to becoming the smallest in the hall. It's a move that we all must make. It's a move that I made too. Long, long ago (twenty years back). Moving to secondary may seem a bit scary, but there's absolutely no need to fear … I'm here to steer you through. Nice to meet you by the way, my name's Christian. I'm a rapper and a teacher, and before that, I was like you: a student.

In this book we're going to look at the whole process of moving up, step by step. We'll start with where you are now, the end of year six, talk about how it feels to leave your primary school, and how to prepare for what's next. The second part of the book is all about the *academic* aspects of year seven. That means the stuff related to your learning. We'll look at what will happen on your first day, the subjects that you'll study, how to find your way around the place, the rules to learn and the new opportunities to pursue. In the third and final part of the book, we're going to talk about you. Yes, you. We're going to talk about life outside of the classroom. That means dealing with friendships, peer pressure, what to do if you see bullying, how to use social media safely when the time comes, healthy relationships and much more.

ARE YOU READY?

ARE YOU SET?

THEN LET'S GO!

↓ SHOUTOUT TO YEAR SIXES

Shoutout to year sixes,

The brilliant bosses of the benches,

Wise storytellers of wild, wicked

adventures,

Rulers of the hall with the measure of the

school,

Everything that you remember is

a treasure full of jewels,

Keep shining when you move...

Shoutout to year sixes,

Conquerors of SATs, fearless finders of

forgotten facts,

You did it with class,

Used scrap paper to show your working

in maths,

Teachers count on you truly,

As you approach the closing credits of

the first movie...

Shoutout to year sixes,

Collectors of memories, creators

of energy,

Fifteen-a-side football games, not one

single referee,

Who cares about the score?

Illustrators of your future, what will

you draw?

Rocketship designers, how high will

you soar?

Shoutout to year sixes,

You navigated primary without a map,

Just like sports day athletics you kept on
track, never fell flat,

Leaping over every hurdle and
still grinning,

You never lost yourselves, so I call that
winning,

As you leap once more towards one more
beginning...

One journey is ending, from primary
school you depart,

But the journey's far from over...

In fact, it's just about to start.

PART 1

YEAR SIX

RUMOURS

Maybe you know some things about secondary schools already, good, exciting things ... or maybe you've heard some things which don't sound so good, maybe there are some rumours going around. There are a lot of rumours and misinformation about secondary schools. The rumours spread because the fear of the unknown is a common sensation. We worry about what it will be like. When lots of people are all worried together, the worries begin to feed each other, until they grow very large indeed. Do not be afraid of wedgies or being expelled for talking. That doesn't happen. Let's take some of the rumours and myths that my year sixes have heard, and address them once and for all.

Myth 1

"The teachers are gonna be horrible, like really strict. We'll get detention all the time."

It's true that secondary schools have different behavioural expectations. As you get older, teachers expect you to act a bit more like adults. Naturally, there will be less tolerance for the type of messing around that you got away with when you were younger. That makes sense though, right? None of this means that you are entering a prison situation, with guards and cells.

Teachers are humans (believe it or not) and have different personalities. Some teachers are stricter than others, just like primary school. Schools have what we call a *behaviour policy* and students are taught exactly what the rules are. If you slip up and get a detention, it's not a disaster, and it doesn't mean that a teacher is horrible, or that you have failed – it's OK – it can happen! All teachers want what's best for you and your education, but sometimes this just means reminding you of expectations.

When I got my first detention, I was terrified! I thought that I'd messed up big time. It brought back the feeling of fear and shame that I used to have in year two, when my teacher, the stern, grandmotherly Mrs Morris, wrote my name on the blackboard, with chalk (old school, I know). The fact is, detentions might happen, and if they do, it's not that disastrous. Just try your best to *do your best*, and that's all you can do.

The teachers at secondary school might seem different to the ones you've known at primary, but they are not. Trust me. I'm both.

Myth 2

"There's gonna be eighteen-year-olds, just like smoking around the place, and they might take my lunch money."

I feel like this happens a lot in American films and cartoons. Some guy called Chad, who has a muscle car, which he probably also calls Chad, pulls up at school, leaps out, and says, "Hey you, you little slimy slug, gimme your lunch money."

Yeah, this doesn't happen in the UK. For a start there's no parking space. Secondly, lunch money isn't really a thing, since most schools operate on a pre-paid system. I understand the fear though. My first time seeing a year six pupil (when in reception) was just like my first time seeing a year thirteen (in year seven). In both cases, they were giants who might tread on me, intentionally or not.

The reality is, in my experience, very different. The year thirteens in secondary school did one of two things: they were either kind to me and helped me with something, or they completely ignored me. Statistically, you are probably more likely to get ignored, but ... oh well. If a year thirteen ever laughs at you, it's because you are travelling at high speed, legs moving like pistons, with an intense expression and a backpack that is an equivalent size to you. At least, when I was in year thirteen, I found that funny, sorry.

As for the smoking, just don't go behind the bike sheds.

Myth 3

"There's gonna be fights all the time."

Secondary schools have more pupils than primary schools do. This does mean it's more likely that people might have disagreements. But that doesn't mean everyone's fighting all the time. When I was a student at secondary school, I saw three fights in seven years – that's not too bad, right? As a teacher at secondary school, I can assure you that any pushing or shoving will be over as soon as it starts; adults are on hand quicker than you can say, "Fight!" because it's our job to keep you safe. The corridors and hallways are not a no-man's-land where no teachers patrol; we're always on the lookout. Schools are places of learning and not training grounds for wrestlers. If you do want to be a wrestler, or the next heavyweight champion of the world, there might be an after-school club for that.

Myth 4

"I'm going to lose my friends when we move school."

I was worried about this when I left primary school. I thought my friendships would suddenly be thrown apart like flimsy boats in a storm, and we'd drift in different directions for ever. However, one of my best friends at primary was called Tom. Tom was cheeky and always had something to say. I would call him the class clown, but clowns aren't funny, and Tom really was (and still is). We left primary school in 2003, a long time before you were born. Now I'm writing this in 2023, and we are still close friends. In fact, I was with Tom today before I wrote this chapter. Our friendship has never drifted apart, and we didn't go to the same secondary school.

My mum says,

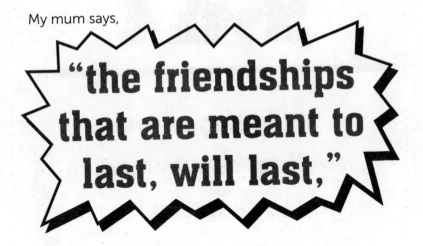

"the friendships
that are meant to
last, will last,"

which is a very *mum* thing to say – but I agree with her.
Perhaps you may lose touch with some of your class,
that's completely natural, but anyone that you want to
stay close to, you'll find a way. For your generation, it's a
lot easier to stay connected than it was for me, because
you have social media (we are going to talk about social
media later, because we need to). Anyway, when it comes
to maintaining friendships, yes, it is more difficult when
you don't see each other every day, but if you want to
keep a friendship, you will be able to. Like most things in
life, it's about putting in the effort. It's worth it. It's a great
feeling to sit with someone and talk about how you met
over twenty-five years ago. For example, in year three,
Tom used to copy my answers in maths, and I let him.
The system worked beautifully until the teacher moved
us apart, and Tom's test results went ... sharply downhill.
Our friendship never did though.

Myth 5

"The lessons are going to be way harder, and we'll get so much homework."

There is some truth in this myth. Some parts of some lessons will be more difficult. But you will also be older, your brain more developed, and your ability to work things out will have improved. I was really worried by the sound of new subjects. In science I had to ask, *what does physics mean? What is chemistry? Biology!?* I thought I'd never get my head round these complicated subjects. It took a bit of time to adjust, but I realized that it wasn't too different from what we were studying in year six. There were just some new terms to learn.

As a teacher, I think lessons must get harder as you progress through school, otherwise you wouldn't progress at all. Think of your brain like a muscle: the more you lift with it, the stronger it gets, as long as your brain (and you) remember to rest as well.

As for homework, well, there's no avoiding it; you are going to have to do some homework. There are certain unavoidable facts in life: Earth orbits the Sun, the Moon controls the tides, water is wet, (healthy) grass is green, (clear) midday skies are blue and ... secondary schools set homework.

Teachers don't want to assign so much homework that it stresses you out. It's meant to be a supplement to your classroom learning. Like a side plate with your main course, to make sure you get enough educational nutrition. Treat homework like broccoli, even if you don't like the taste. Trust me, you'll be better off having it.

Of course, we all have different homes. When I was a teenager at home, I felt my home didn't work as well as other kids at my school, and that made it harder to do homework. During my parents' divorce, I found it difficult to do homework, because my home was louder; there were arguments, reactions, and distractions. I didn't sleep as much, and it was a lot harder to concentrate because I felt upset. Teachers asked, "Christian, why aren't you doing your homework? It used to be on time!?"

I didn't know what to say. Now, as an adult, I am always thinking about how students' homes are working, and how that might impact something like homework, so don't worry if there are reasons that you are struggling. And if you are struggling, do what I didn't do and tell the teacher. We are more understanding than you think. You never know, we might have experienced some of it ourselves.

So, there are five myths, and hopefully they've been busted. But just in case you need a reminder not to listen to all the rumours, let's put it in a rap.

I HEARD THIS RUMOUR, YEAH

I heard this rumour, yeah,
That the headteacher is a villain,
Her blood runs cold, and I've been told,
That when she shouts it's chilling.

I heard this rumour, yeah,
And it's one that I should mention,
That if you're not silent, it all gets violent,
And you're slammed into detention.

I heard this rumour, yeah,
The playground is the Wild West,
There are duels at school, it all
gets cruel,
So, hide under your desk.

My teacher heard these rumours,
That swirled around my head,
"It's not true, that's not what
they do!"
Now, finally the truth was said!

THE FINAL COUNTDOWN

While the rampant rumours running around can make the transition to secondary school a bit frightening, let's also consider just how exciting the final term is. There is a certain indescribable atmosphere that I will try and describe anyway: it's a feeling that you are on the edge of a great adventure, like an astronaut aboard a rocket ship, heart beating quicker as the countdown begins, ready to explore parts of the Universe you haven't yet encountered.

So, enjoy the last term and savour it. Even in Britain, the weather should be sunnier, the days brighter and longer and the playground games played with an urgent energy. Everything feels alive with possibility. Even that strict teacher you've been afraid of for six years might just crack a rare smile. You never know.

As the end of term approaches you should write those sweet thank-you messages to your teachers and have a bit of sugary lemonade at the summer party before demonstrating your best dance moves, which definitely aren't as good as you think they are (unless that just goes for me). Maybe your school has a prom, in which case, that's your chance to dress up and be glamorous for the cameras. It's also time to get involved in your leavers' assembly. A leavers' assembly is what we call a rite of passage. That means a ceremony or event marking a significant stage in someone's life.

Basically, it's a really BIG moment.

This usually happens on your last day. The last day is something that you think you're ready for, but when it arrives, the waves of emotion can be really powerful, so if those feelings flood you, don't swim against the currents and try to hold back the tears, just go with the flow. You all rush like an incoming tide through the school gates in the morning, knowing that it is the beginning of the end, and the end of the beginning.

There you are. About to leave year six. Strutting confidently in your *Clarks* shoes, laces in a neat bow, white shirt, heart drumming an excited percussive pattern on your ribcage. No doubt there are butterflies performing acrobatics in your stomach, and a fluttering sensation of nerves and excitement. There were for me back then. For the last time you are year sixes, nearly as tall as the teacher, voices booming loud, shoulders back ... you are at the peak of your purposeful power.

Then the goodbyes get underway. Glittering gel pens, fluorescent highlighters, and chunky marker pens in hand, you begin to write, not on paper, but on those clean white shirts. There's a scraping, tickling feeling of those pens on your shoulder blades, as your friends scribe their fond farewells into the fibre of your shirt. The messages on shirts don't change much through the ages. *Miss you. Good luck. Legend. Kick me.* You will wear those shirts with pride.

The last day tends to pass fast in a busy blur of noise and emotion. Then you filter into the assembly hall, to take your places on the throne-like benches for your leavers' assembly. The assembly is a chance to reminisce on the years that you've shared together as a year group, and to look forward to the future. No doubt you'll sing a well-rehearsed anthem too. Parents and guardians line the edges of the hall, united in disbelief that the years have passed at such a speed, remembering you in reception, and marvelling at the power of the whirlwind that has transported you here. There are tearful faces everywhere you look. But that's okay. It's never a bad thing to cry, especially these tears of joy and triumph, celebrating all that you have achieved. Once you dry your eyes, start envisioning the next stage of school, because that's where you're heading...

Get ready for the countdown, you're about to move up!

YOU HAVE THE POTENTIAL OF...

The first step of a journey,

The kick off of a match,

The first verse of a poem,

Or a plan about to hatch.

A sprinter crouching on the tracks,

A key in the ignition,

A slingshot pulled back to the max,

The briefing of a mission.

The revving of an engine,

Which is gearing up to roar,

A plane upon the runway,

Or a bird about to soar.

A helicopter's rotor-blade,

Starting to rotate,

Or a text that you've been waiting for,

As you feel your phone vibrate.

An arrow in the archer's bow,

A tightly coiled spring,

The first shot of a movie,

You've been waiting to begin.

You have the potential of an astronaut,

In the countdown of a launch,

Or a year six leaving primary,

With a new universe to explore…

UNIFORMS FOR SEPTEMBER

The summer before year seven is a waiting period. A stage of inbetween-ness. Caught between two worlds, like a rocket that drifts through deep space; a long way from familiar Earth but not yet touched down on a new planet.

At the start of the summer holidays, September is a distant shape on the horizon, but the closer you get, the larger it looms. Suddenly, September is all you can see. The back-to-school adverts begin to show on the TV and the hands on the clock seem to turn at a faster rate. You are told things you don't want to know, like the price of a tie.

As the summer deepens, it's impossible to ignore those back-to-school adverts because you need a uniform, and the uniforms at secondary school aren't quite the same as primary. At primary, my mate Johnny wore his grey shorts all year round. Heavy rain in January, shorts. Hailstones the size of his head in February, shorts. Sunshine in June, shorts (fair enough). Snow in December, school got cancelled but I bet Johnny was at home, throwing snowballs, wearing shorts. One time his mum forced him to wear trousers and they got ripped by morning break. Johnny had a sharp shock at secondary school because you can't simply show up in shorts. First item to buy: trousers.

This was my shopping list for secondary school uniform, and yours will probably look similar.

SHOES, BLACK WITH NO LOGOS

Most kids try to buy black sports trainers and say they are school shoes, but lots of schools have got wise to this and banned trainers.

RUCKSACK, BLACK OR GREY, LOGOS ALLOWED

I had the same rucksack for three years until it got so worn down the straps fell off and the zip with its many broken teeth urgently needed some sort of bag dentist. Make sure you have a very strong bag because it's going to be full of stuff. When you carry your bag around, only carry what you need for the day, not for the whole week, or you won't be able to move. You're not going backpacking around Australia.

TIE

Mine was red, but yours may be any colour. I had to learn to tie it, I spent a fair bit of August in the mirror feeling foolish. Tying myself in knots. It was too short, then too long, then too fat, then too thin. Eventually I got it, just about; perseverance is the key. If you need help with yours, then you can ask somebody that you live with, or use a very valuable tool called YouTube. If you want an even easier option, you can cheat a bit and get a clip-on tie!

WHITE SHIRT (x4)

Get a few of these if you can because if you put a pen in your pocket, it will leak at some point, and you'll end up with blotches and stains.

TROUSERS

You can't wear shorts. Ever. Grey or black trousers only. Girls get the choice between trousers or a skirt.

JUMPER

Mine was an uninspiring grey, but yours might be a more exciting colour. Apple green? Tomato ketchup red?

BLAZER

A blazer is one of the major changes from your primary wardrobe. It makes you feel grown up when you put one on for the first time. You brush your shoulders off feeling like a hot shot. Make sure you get the right size and it's not too big, otherwise you might look a bit like a wizard. Unluckily for me, I remember disliking my blazer because it had a fluorescent, bright yellow outline, and other schools made fun of that, saying that we looked like wasps, which stung a bit. I'm sure you'll be more fortunate.

SOCKS, ANY TYPE YOU LIKE

The only way to express our individuality was through our socks, but for the sake of ease, I just wore grey ones.

Uniform exceptions are made for extreme weather, for example, you'll be able to take your blazers off on hot days, (but still no shorts!), and when it's freezing cold in winter, girls can exchange skirts for trousers.

As you'll notice, most uniforms are not very colourful. The point of a uniform is not to be loud, extravagant or showy, but to establish a sense of shared belonging. Uniforms promote the values of a school; they might have a school crest or an inspirational motto, which reminds you why you are there.

IT'S IMPORTANT TO FEEL LIKE YOU BELONG, LIKE YOU ARE A PART OF SOMETHING

LARGER THAN YOURSELF

School uniforms also create a level playing field, they keep everybody equal. This means that you don't have to worry about having the latest Jordans on your feet, that would be way too stressful! It doesn't matter how much money you have when it comes to uniforms. Uniforms mean that you don't have to overthink what you wear each day, so you can spend more time thinking about what really matters.

There are rules in place which mean schools should have uniform policies that are as inclusive as possible. School uniforms will not be too costly, they are meant to be affordable, comfortable and appropriate for everyone. No one should be made to feel 'left out' or uncomfortable by what they are asked to wear. Uniform polices should not discriminate against any student on the basis of their gender, race or religion. There are also guidelines to prevent 'hair discrimination' because, for some people, certain hairstyles can represent who they are, their heritage and their cultural values. A school policy that just bans certain hairstyles without thinking of the impact on different races or religions is an unfair one. For example, pupils should not be forbidden from wearing head coverings, braids, locs, twists, plaits, cornrows and Afro hairstyles. Nearly all schools have uniforms, but not every single one. There are different attitudes around uniforms. Some students prefer them because it's easier to wear the same outfit as everyone else, every day. Other students don't like having uniforms because it makes it hard to express who you are via your appearance. Yet, even with a school uniform, you are so brilliantly individual that you can communicate your uniqueness in many other ways. By the way, don't forget your PE kit, because your usual white, buttoned shirt won't look too good in the mud! Get a strong sports bag to keep your PE stuff in too, you don't want your football boots on your shiny new books. Schools won't ask you to get a lot of complicated gear for PE, there's no need for ice skates or a wetsuit, it will just be the standard stuff, so it will be affordable. Once you've got that, then you're all kitted out.

During the holidays, take a trip to a stationery shop, pick out a pencil case and pack it with all that you need. At primary school, all the stationery is provided. Secondary school is BYOB (Bring Your Own Biros) and other equipment. Here's a recommended checklist of what to get. You don't need to buy absolutely everything on the list, don't worry – it's just a guide for what is useful to have.

GENERAL SUPPLIES

- Pencil case

- Blue/black biro pens

- Handwriting pen (fountain pen with ink cartridges)

- Highlighters (try to get four different colours)

- HB pencils

- Eraser

- 30cm ruler (get a foldable one so it doesn't snap and it fits in your pencil case)

- Ink eraser/correction fluid

MATHS SUPPLIES

- A compass (one with a point, not one for finding North)
- A 360 degree protractor
- A set square
- A scientific calculator (not to be used to try and write rude words or emojis with the numbers)

ENGLISH AND MODERN FOREIGN LANGUAGES SUPPLIES

....

- Dictionary/thesaurus

  (get a foreign language dictionary too,

  depending on what language you study)

ART SUPPLIES

- A glue stick
- A pair of scissors
- Colouring pencils

ICT SUPPLIES

- A USB stick
- Headphones

You don't need to buy a laptop!

Okay, that pencil case is pretty full now right. As the first day approaches, pack your bag the night before, you don't want to be doing it in a mad rush with a mouthful of toast. Make sure you've got the stationery you need in your pencil case. "Can I borrow a pen?" is a phrase often heard at secondary, but you don't want to be the one always saying it. With your bag packed, go to bed early, so you're on your best form. Rest your head on the pillow and get ready to dive into your dreams. Tomorrow is a big day.

BRING ON YEAR SEVEN.

PART 2

YEAR SEVEN

THE
FIRST DAY

THERE ARE MORE REASONS TO BE EXCITED THAN NERVOUS

It's the moment you've all been waiting for. Waking up on that first day, it's fine if your feelings see-saw between anxiety on one side and enthusiastic excitement on the other. There's probably an even balance of the two. That's cool, it's certainly how I felt. But trust me, I think there are more reasons to be excited than nervous. You'll put your uniform on, including that brand new blazer, check in the mirror, and feel like a boss. There'll be a rush that moves through your body, as you're filled with a cool, calm confidence, a sensation that seems to say, "I've got this!" Make sure you have breakfast. It's a big day. Your family will want a photo, so pose for a moment, smile to the click of the camera, swing your rucksack on your back, then walk out your front door.

There is a Charles Dickens book that you might study in secondary school called *A Christmas Carol*. In the story there is a character called the 'Ghost of Christmas Past', who is described as being immeasurably ancient, and indescribably young at the same time. A combination of experienced wisdom and youthful innocence. Well, that's exactly how you'll feel. Old and young at the same time. Old because you're independent now and you've learned to tie a tie. But young too. Young because you're entering the lowest year group in the school, in terms of age and experience. You've got a lot to learn, but it's going to be fun! So, when you arrive at school, walk through those metal gates like you're made of iron. You've got this.

This probably won't be the first time that you've visited the school, because you might have had an induction or an open day before starting. However, you're not expected to know your way around yet. So when you walk through the gate, your new teachers will be on hand to show you where to go. There will be a hubbub of excited chatter, as the meetings and greetings take place. Over the noise, sometimes a teacher will have a megaphone to amplify their voice, and they'll be saying in a commanding tone, "Year seven, come this wayyyyyy!" You will line up with your class or form, shuffling with expectant energy. The noise quiets as you listen for instructions. What's going to happen next? You might be arranged in alphabetical order. My surname begins with F, so on my first day, the first kids I met were either side of me in the line, with surnames beginning with E or G.

You might already know some people in the line from primary school or induction days, or everyone might be completely new, but don't worry – they won't be strangers for long. It's an exciting feeling to look up and down the line of your class and wonder, *who will become the friends to help shape the next six years?* Then, with a word from a teacher, the line starts to move as one, with increasing speed and motion, like a train leaving the station, and your destination is probably to a welcome assembly. Full steam ahead. In the assembly, the headteacher will address you all as a year group and congratulate you on how smart you look. Look around the room, you're all going through the same emotions.

Every single stranger sitting in that room is a potential best friend.

That's an exciting thought. After the assembly, the line reforms and departs, this time for your form room. You will meet your form tutor, who is the teacher that will be with you all year. Form tutors have a pastoral role for you, that means they look after your wellbeing, and make sure you are happy and everything is okay. On your first day, they might run some icebreaker activities, to help you get to know one another.

Here's an icebreaker question that you can ask your new classmates:

Can you tell me two truths and one lie, and I have to guess which is which?

This would be my response, see if you can guess, which one is a lie:

1) The rapper 50 Cent likes the way I teach and posted a video about me saying that.

2) I became a teacher because I got a knee injury and couldn't play professional football anymore.

3) I wrote my first poem (that I can remember) in Year 5.

Did you guess the lie? It was number two. I never got close to a high level of football, although not for lack of trying. Plus, I love teaching and I'd never want to do anything else. The other statements were completely true!

Let's try some more icebreaker questions...

- **What's your favourite YouTube channel?**

- **If you could you go anywhere in the world, where would you go?**

- **If you could have any superpower, what would it be and why?**

- **What celebrities would you ask to visit our school?**

- **If you won a million pounds, what would you buy?**

Icebreaker questions are designed to start conversations, and through conversations, you'll get to know your classmates. Maybe you can even tell them a fact. Ask them who invented the phrase to break the ice. I bet they don't know. The answer is William Shakespeare. You're welcome.

After the ice has melted faster than a Solero in the Sahara, it's time to leave the form room, you'll line up once more, and you'll be heading for the classrooms, together with classmates you already know a little better, where all types of subjects await you.

61

SUBJECTS

In year six, you probably had one classroom, and you stayed there with your teacher all day. Yes, you go into the school hall for assemblies, or outside for PE, but generally, there's not too much travelling. In year seven, it's very different. The only room you'll go to every day is your form room. You'll go there in the morning for registration. Then again for another registration after lunch. Apart from that, you're on the move. You become nomadic. You'll get given a timetable.

To me, the whole thing looked like a puzzle.

I couldn't put the pieces together, but you might find yours easy to decode. This is another difference to primary school – there are a lot more subjects to study.

Let's do an activity – I've made a list of all the subjects that were on my timetable. Yours will look similar. On the next page there's a rap, where each line references a different subject. Can you match the rap line to the correct subject?

MATCH THE SUBJECTS

I stay composed like Mozart, mate **1**
Make the earth shake like tectonic plates **2**
Never at fault, run tracks, I'm Usain Bolt **3**
I can measure lightning in electric volts **4**

Je suis un professeur de rap **5**
Learn to write code to compute my facts **6**
Paint like Picasso put a pattern to a page **7**
Deliver dramatic monologues on the stage **8**

Picking through poems, analyse novels **9**
Learn how Genghis Khan never grovelled **10**
Study our society, democratic ideals **11**
Who worships who? How do they feel? **12**

Draw it on the paper, build your design **13**
Don't ask y but x you have to find! **14**

English
Maths
Science
MFL (Modern Foreign Languages)
Design & Technology

Music
Physical Education (PE)
Information & Communication Technology (ICT)
Art

Religious Education/ Religious Studies (RE/RS)
Citizenship
Geography
History
Drama

MATCH THE SUBJECTS (ANSWERS)

1. Music
2. Geography
3. Physical Education (PE)
4. Science
5. MFL (Modern Foreign Languages)
6. Information & Communication Technology (ICT)
7. Art
8. Drama
9. English
10. History
11. Citizenship
12. Religious Education/ Religious Studies (RE/RS)
13. Design & Technology
14. Maths

How many did you get right? All of them? Thought so, well done. Now, all of these new subjects generated different feelings for me. Some, I instinctively thought I would like, and others I was more worried about. It will probably be the same with you. We all have different interests and we are drawn towards certain activities more than others, or maybe you just love everything! Go, you! Let me give you some explanations of some of the new subjects, so you a know a little bit about what to expect.

MUSIC

This lesson is unrecognizable from how it might have been in primary, where you probably had sword fights with recorders and occasionally used them to make something resembling a song. In my primary,

one boy claimed to be able to play the recorder with his nose,

which sounds as disgusting as it was untrue.

Moving up to secondary school, in year seven, my future was a mystery, I had no idea that I would become a rapper in later life and that music would be very important to me.

Our music lessons were not like they are now. It felt like we sat around on keyboards and aimlessly plonked around unsuccessfully on the keys for the most part, much to the annoyance of our teacher, Mr Something.

Music nowadays is not a case of just sitting around at a keyboard and pressing buttons at random. Today, you can make use of technology, and you can make hip-hop beats on a DAW (Digital Audio Workspace) just as easily as picking up a clarinet. You can learn about classical and contemporary (modern) music in the same classroom.

Some schools have large music departments with lots of musical instruments to choose from, other schools might have a smaller selection (but there will definitely be keyboards). There will be opportunities to join a band, or to get involved with singing lessons in choir ... maybe even hit the drums as hard as you can in a soundproof studio, a great way to relieve stress.

The curriculum for music in year seven picks up from where you left it in year six – it involves a combination of singing, listening, composing and performing. There are also musical terms to learn. Do you know your pitch from your tempo? You soon will. Music is an amazing way to express yourself and to translate your inner emotions into a creative form for others to hear. So whatever tool or instrument you choose, make some hits!

DRAMA

Drama at primary school was essentially the school play. We did a school play every year, and my main role was a goose in Mother Goose.

In year seven, our drama teacher Miss Something was, like most drama teachers, very dramatic. I really liked her. She had a lot of energy. In this lesson, expect movement – I doubt that you'll be standing still.

Unless you are pretending to be a rock.

Also, expect fun. Drama is a great laugh and a chance to create all sorts of inventive characters. It's also a brilliant mode of communication, sometimes by pretending to be somebody else, we can also communicate how we personally feel.

Drama involves a lot of group work, so be prepared to work as a team. There are many different ways to contribute to a performance. You don't have to be the main star, you can direct, you can be a stage hand and do the heavy lifting.

All roles are important.

Can you hear me at the back? Drama also focuses on how to project your voice, and to make yourself heard. An essential skill in life. If thou art concerned that drama will just be about Shakespeare, then fear not, it isn't!

My only advice is try not to just stand around and act cool — that's boring (and uncool). You get out of drama what you put in, and even if you are naturally quiet and shy, that's OK. Just give it a go, and you might surprise yourself. This isn't a lesson where you sit around cross-legged and read dust-speckled scripts. This is a lesson that gets you on your feet. Get to it! Who's gonna win the Oscar first?

MODERN FOREIGN LANGUAGES

Secondary schools offer a choice of modern foreign languages. Generally these include French, Spanish, German and perhaps Italian. Some schools even offer less-modern foreign languages, like Latin (Latin would be a DFL: dead foreign language). In year seven we studied French, and the teacher, Monsieur Quelque-Chose, was a bit of a legend. I say this because he used to show us a lot of French comedy films. I couldn't understand too much of what was going on, but they seemed funny. This might not happen often in your MFL lessons but I'm sure they will be fun regardless.

MFL lessons focus on the development of four skills: listening, speaking, reading and writing. You will also expand your vocabularies, by learning how to say more and more words. Also, you'll learn correct grammar. Grammar might not sound super exciting, but being able to properly communicate in a second language actually is.

This is because learning a language is like learning to see the world through another person's eyes.

Seeing the world in this way helps us to understand other people's perspectives and points of view. This makes for a world more full of empathy. Empathy is the ability to put yourself in someone's place and understand how they feel. It's good to be empathetic and learning a language promotes this. So maybe you should really pay attention in these classes (like all of your classes) because being bilingual is awesome. Don't be scared of seeming silly; get talking.

DESIGN AND TECHNOLOGY

I am not a very practical person, which meant I struggled with Design and Technology at secondary school. In the first lesson we had to make a wooden box, and my box was wonky, it looked more like one of Mother Goose's eggs, but it didn't matter. I tried my best. That's what it's all about.

DT involves a mix of different disciplines, there's a bit of science, a bit of maths, a bit of computing, and also some art. In the lessons, there are three main stages to DT:

1) **Design** – This involves creating sketches and plans of a product, either by hand or on computer.

2) **Make** – This is where you use the tools in the classroom to create your product and bring it to life!

3) **Evaluate** – This is where you reflect on what you (and other people) have made, and you think about the impact that technology has on society.

DT is a really fun subject and allows you to express yourself in what you create. I loved the smell of wood in the workshop, the sensation of soft sawdust on the soles of my shoes, even though I couldn't saw straight. My advice in DT is to do everything gradually, carefully and with precision. You need to be safe. For example, take off your tie ... you don't want it getting caught in the sander. When you're making something, you get to wear goggles and a lab coat and it feels oh so professional. So, once you're kitted out and doing everything safely, start building...

What will you make? Impress me.

P.S. Some schools offer food technology as part of this subject. This is where you get your aprons on and learn how to cook, and

you get to annoy your parents by asking them at the last minute for a bunch of ingredients you need to bring in to school.

My mum really hated trying to urgently find onions at 7.30am.

INFORMATION COMMUNICATION TECHNOLOGY

Do you know your hardware from your software? I barely do. You probably know more about computers than I do. I never understood how they worked, and still don't. I guarantee my ICT classes will have been nothing like yours in year seven. Technology has moved on. We sat around on Microsoft Excel trying to pretend we knew what we were doing. Computers, like you, the next generation, will control the direction of our planet's future – so this lesson is really important. You will learn the meaning of words like algorithm. Trust me, that's an important one to know. You will also learn to write computer programs to solve problems, that sounds quite cool to be honest. ICT will take place in a computer suite which sounds fancy, and you will sit in front of a computer and do what I never could: learn how they work. Learning how computers work is only part of it though, you will also learn how to use technology safely, and protect your privacy and identity online. This is more important than ever. So, in a responsible way, get clicking on that mouse, and embark on your mission to decode the future.

OTHER SUBJECTS

Other subjects that you have studied before will get a glow up. They will reappear in a newer, shinier form.

ENGLISH

This was my favourite subject at school. That's probably no surprise as I'm writing a book right now. I had a team of amazing English teachers that helped to change my life, by encouraging me to follow my dreams and become a poet and rapper!

This subject helps you to communicate fluently, so that you can express your ideas and emotions to others through their reading and listening. The realm of reading and writing is defined as literacy. The skill of speaking is defined as oracy. Both oracy and literacy are hugely important because they help you to express yourself, to be heard and understood. It is a way of finding your voice.

In English lessons you will develop your skills in four main areas:

1. **Reading**

2. **Writing**

3. **Speaking**

4. **Grammar/vocabulary**

You'll read works of literature that are composed of fiction (imaginary) and non-fiction (factual). You'll read whole books, plays and poems. You'll read from a range of historical periods and geographical locations, and in the process you'll learn about the world, and yourself too.

THE MORE YOU READ, THE BETTER YOU WRITE.

The more words you have for fluent speech, the better you can structure your thoughts into increasingly complex sentences. Do you know the longest word in the English language? What is:

pneumonoultramicroscopicsilicovolcanoconiosis?[1]

How's your spelling? Do you know the difference between grammar and Grandma? This is your chance. English is not dead and dusty. It's vital and alive. Who knows, maybe you'll write a book too. I'll watch this space.

SCIENCE

The science curriculum is split into three parts. Biology, chemistry and physics. In biology, you get to wear a lab coat and goggles again (looking oh so scientific). If your biology classes are like mine were, then you might even get to dissect (cut up and study) a pig's heart ... it's kind of gruesome but very, very interesting. You'll want to wash your hands. (Also, this is optional so if you want to sit it out, you can – don't worry!)

[1] It's a name for a type of lung disease caused by inhaling very fine particles of volcanic ash and sand dust.

Biology is all about living organisms, meaning plants and animals – and how they work, inside and out. For animals, you'll learn about cells and skeletons, nutrition and digestion, health and reproduction. For plants, maybe you have one in your house, have you ever seen it turn towards the sunlight? Why does it do that? In biology you'll find out. You'll also learn how to look after the habitats and ecosystems of our changing world. Important stuff!

In chemistry, I remember the fire. Literally. You attach a Bunsen burner to a gas tap with a rubber tube, turn it on and whoosh, a burst of orange flame. It's very cool (but not in terms of temperature). What's the Universe made of? If you're interested in that question, then in chemistry, you'll be in your element. What's an element? You'll find that out too.

In one of our first chemistry lessons we dropped a tiny of nugget of soluble lithium into a beaker of water. The way it behaved reminded me of a year seven student. Dropped into a new environment, the lithium was still for a nanosecond, then all of a sudden, it fizzed around, exploring everywhere it could at high speed. That's what your first few weeks will probably be like (although I hope you won't dissolve at the end).

Then there's physics. Physics is all about the invisible

forces that control our Universe and the beings in it. That includes you. Maybe you'll be the next Einstein.

What does E = mc² mean? Was the Big Bang really that big? What happens when you split an atom? How fast is lightspeed? What time is lunch?

All of those questions get asked in physics, only one of them has the answer: 12.30pm. I also recall one morning, when my friend Jacob fell off his chair after leaning back on it, the physics teacher angrily asked him, "How did that happen!?" Jacob replied, "It was gravity, sir." At least he was paying attention.

HISTORY

You studied history a little bit in primary school. But that's in the past now. The subject is different when you get to secondary. You go into much more depth and detail. You'll learn terms like primary and secondary source. This is nothing to do with Ketchup and HP. The KS3 curriculum that you will study in year seven is a mix of British history, and the history of the wider world. You will study the story of Britain as a chronological narrative. That means in order of time, starting with the earliest times, all the way up to present day. It's a fascinating story. It's not just a list of dead kings and queens. There are many things to discover. What was *Magna Carta*? What caused the Black Death? Why did the peasants revolt? How long was the Hundred Years' War? Okay, you should get the last one.[2]

---

[2] If you said 100 years, you'd be wrong! It actually went on for 116 years. But that was a slightly less catchy name. Good fact to try and catch out your friends (or your history teacher), though.

History isn't just about what happened, it's about how it happened and why. And no one seems to agree on any of it. There are many different arguments and viewpoints to sift through, before forming your own opinion. Understanding the past helps us to understand the present, so you shouldn't think of history of something that is over and done.

It's still happening right now. You never know, you might make history yourself one day.

GEOGRAPHY

Have you ever wondered if mountains could move? Where does the lava end up when a volcano erupts? This is the subject for you. Geography is about the world and its people. Geography is divided into two categories, physical and human. Physical geography refers to the shifting tectonic plates beneath our feet, the slithering, icy glaciers slipping downhill, the wild waves that roar like thunder and smash into the rocks of the coast. Stuff like that. It's exciting. You also get to go on field trips, which aren't actually trips to a field – they are more interesting than that. Human geography is about us and what we do while we live on this planet. What does population mean? What is urbanization? You'll find out. Humans have an undeniable impact on our world, and our planet is changing quickly – geography is a way of understanding what's going on, and what we can do to preserve the place that gives us life. It doesn't get more meaningful than that.

RELIGIOUS EDUCATION/ RELIGIOUS STUDIES/ CITIZENSHIP/ PSHE

Some secondary schools in the UK are faith schools. This means that religion is central to everyday life in the school. Other schools are secular. That means that religion does not feature in the school at all. However, there will be the chance to learn about religions. In religious studies or religious education (some schools give it a different name) you learn about people's different beliefs.

In a multicultural place like Britain, this is a really important subject.

There are many faiths to be found in Britain, including: Christianity, Islam, Hinduism, Judaism, Sikhism and Buddhism. Being knowledgeable about how people worship, and the principles by which they live their life, helps us to understand one another, and build a more tolerant country.

You will study the country in a subject called *citizenship*. In this lesson, you learn about how our society is structured. What does it mean to be a citizen? What is the role of parliament? What are the laws of the land?

These questions will be answered and more. Here, you'll learn about the political system in the UK. We are a democracy, that means everybody is entitled to have a say in how we are governed. You can participate in politics by voting (once you turn eighteen).

It's good to make informed decisions, which means you should make a good decision to get informed!

Citizenship will help you with that.

Then there's PSHE. That stands for personal, social, health and economic education. PSHE is a non-statutory subject, which means it does not have to be taught in a certain way; teachers and schools can decide how it is taught, and what is covered. Although PSHE is technically optional, the National Curriculum states, "All schools should study PSHE". It is an essential subject because it helps you to think about your own life and the choices that you make. The main topics that come up in PSHE lessons include: education about drugs, relationships and sex education, financial education and the importance of physical activity for a healthy lifestyle.

PHYSICAL EDUCATION (PE)

Do you want to be the next Emma Raducanu or Andy Murray? Do you have Premier League dreams? Gold medal aspirations? Olympic ambitions? Or do you just want to have fun with your mates running around a muddy field? This is the lesson for you. Physical education is all about getting active. You learn to compete in a wide range of sports, whilst also gaining an understand of the long term health benefits of exercise. The National Curriculum says you will "use a range of tactics to overcome opponents through team and individual games". This is all sounds very strategic and dramatic but remember, it's not about the winning, it's the taking part that counts! So what sports will you be taking part in? You've got athletics, basketball, badminton, cricket, cross country, dodgeball, football, hockey, netball, rounders, rugby, tennis, gymnastics and more! Get involved and hone your skills until you become a masterful artist out there on the field.

ART AND DESIGN

My art teacher, let's call him Mr Brush, used to say, "You can't go wrong with art." I used to look at my paintings and think, *I've definitely gone wrong*. Why did my vase look more like a wobbly Pringles can? Why did my sunrise look like an upturned bowl of porridge? Despite my lack of natural talent, I loved art and design. It's a lesson that is all about self-expression. Plus Mr Brush never said shush, we were allowed to talk freely, and it was a great way to have conversations over paint palettes.

Do you know your Van Gogh from your Picasso? Your Monet from your Manet? I didn't either, but it was really enjoyable to learn about these artists, some of whom had very colourful lives, and to try replicate their styles. It's not just about painting, you draw in sketchbooks, sculpt with clay and generally just have a messy, creative hour to feel free!

MATHS

Let's not forget more of the core subjects. Maths is a discipline that has been millennia in the making, providing the solutions to some of history's most puzzling problems, or problematic puzzles. It was maths that put man on the Moon in 1969. Although it was termed 'man on the Moon' – it was all made possible by a woman. American mathematician, Katherine Johnson, did all the calculations by hand on stacks upon stacks of paper.

Her knowledge was literally out of this world.

You can't have science without maths. You can't have technology without maths. You can't have engineering without maths. You can't buy an ice cream without maths. You get the idea. Unlike some subjects, there's always a correct answer in maths. Two plus two never equals five. Some students like that fact, that maths behaves in a predictable way, for other students, like me at school, it can make maths more difficult. I struggled with maths at school, but now I have come to appreciate it. I know now how important it is. Important enough to write a rap about it...

MATHS

Maths is more than algebra in fact,
It's Y we can find X on the map,
When we look 4 buried treasure,
We need 2 be exact,
Maths is the tool that can help us with that.

Maths is what put man upon the Moon,
A woman named Katherine came up with
the rules[3],
She did the calculations and she had 2 get
them right,
Otherwise the rocket ship would never
take flight.

So you can't really claim that the limit is the sky,
Because maths is the subject that helps us 2 fly,
Higher than the Shard, even higher 2 to the stars,
Give me a high 5 now I've rapped all the bars.

[3] Katherine Johnson was a mathematician and NASA scientist from the United States. She worked on the calculations that made the 1969 Moon landings possible.

Quick maths – find the numbers that I mentioned in the rap and add them together, what do you get?* Did you get it right? Maths is your chance to know your decimals, fractions, percentages, shapes, graphs and more. It's time to become a problem solver or even a rocket scientist.

Maybe you'll write the code to get us to Mars?

SUBJECT SUMMARY

From all the subjects listed above, you will have favourites, and ones that you find less enjoyable, it's a matter of personal preference. Yet, regardless of which ones you like best, every single subject at school has something essential for you, so...

*The answer is 17.

GO IN WITH AN OPEN MIND, AND YOU NEVER KNOW WHAT YOU'LL FIND.

LOSING YOUR WAY/FINDING A PLACE

On our first day, once we reached our form room, we were given planners. Planners, as the name suggests, were to help us plan. A planner was not a personal assistant who followed us around with information, reminders and directions. That would have been nice, but instead it was just a little, laminated paper book. You can use this planner to write down your homework which I really recommend, with so much going on, it's easy to forget stuff. On the first page of the book there is a timetable. The school day is separated into time periods and the timetable is slightly different each day of the week, so that all subjects are covered.

Having the timetable in your hand is just the beginning. Before you can start these new lessons, you'll need to navigate the unfamiliar environment of the school and actually find your way to the classrooms and lunch hall. Each school day will have a break (it's no longer called playtime) and a lunch time. At lunch time (if you don't bring food from home), be prepared that the queue for a meal is not the most orderly of lines, it involves lots of hungry students jostling for their food. There will be teachers on hand to act as crowd control though. You can have hot or cold food, and generally there is a pre-payment system, where you can load money onto a card, or even your fingerprint. Be kind and polite to the dinner staff, because they are definitely people you want to keep on your side. You don't have to stay with your class at lunch, you can go anywhere you like, in the canteen or playground. Lunch times can feel very busy, but make sure you have time to eat, because that's much-needed fuel for learning.

Speaking of learning, beside each subject on my timetable there was a code in brackets (EN5, SB6 etc). What did that mean? That was the location of the lesson. Secondary schools are arranged in departments. Usually, all of the English lessons will be in the English block, all of the science lessons will be in the science block and so on. Sometimes these departments were nearby to one another, sometimes they seemed ages away. Be prepared to up your step count. You'll probably only have about five minutes for changeover between lessons. During changeover, you'll see rivers of students flowing this way and that, moving into smaller streams and then siphoning into classrooms. Don't try go against the flow as you'll bump into people, generally sticking to the left hand side is a good idea. Depending on the lesson location, we'd be moving at a gentle stroll, a mild trot or a full on sprint. In my school, we learned that it was a ten-minute walk from maths to PE, but we only had five minutes in between classes to make the journey, so PE started a bit early: we had to run there.

LOST

The ringing bell is a starter pistol,
Everyone sprints some place at pace,
It's chaos and carnage in the chase,
Whether you like it or not, you're in the race,
Backpack strapped to your shoulder blades,
RUN! COME ON, RUN!

But where's the finish line? What's the class?
You've lost your mates and you've lost track,
You're in the maze, without a map,
Do you go forward or retrace back?
You need science but you're outside maths,
RUN! COME ON, RUN!

Then some good luck from out the blue,
The science block comes into view,
You bet everyone's there but you…
You pant into the room … out of breath …
and cough,
But the teacher says…
"Ah, you're the first one here, everyone else
is lost!"

I based that poem on a true story, and it just goes to show that you never need to panic, because everyone else is in the same situation as you. Never be afraid to ask for help or directions. Teachers and other students expect it. For me, it took about a term to find where everything was. This will probably be the case for you. On your first day, find out where the toilets are, where the school office is and if there is a locker room, because you might not want to carry your coat around.

Finding your way around might seem daunting. But treat it like an adventure. Maybe you'll be given a map, except the buried treasure you have to find is algebra in maths. X marks the spot. Secondary schools are larger than primary schools in every way, and that includes the area they cover, but don't worry, making your way around gets easier by the day. You might be given an orienteering session, which sounds exciting. 'Orienteering' sounds like you'll be learning how to read a compass, find the North Star, build an igloo and win the race to the South Pole. But it's not that. However, it will be very useful, and will help you map the layout of the school.

At the start, you'll probably get lost once or twice at your new school; I definitely did ... (as did my whole class) but you'll get your bearings. If you do get lost and end up being late for lessons...

DON'T PANIC.

Teachers expect this from year sevens in the first term and won't mind, but if you're still doing it in year thirteen, they might think that you're getting lost on purpose.

Yet, it's not just a case of getting around the school, but also getting to it. You have to make a new journey to and from school. In some parts of the world this journey can involve the perilous crossing of mountains, contending with crocodiles in rapid rivers or walking for many miles. My grandma told me that in the 1930s she walked six miles to school each morning, in the countryside of Ireland, with potatoes in her pockets to keep her hands warm. I don't know if she made the potato bit up. I imagine your journey won't be as long, and won't involve mountains, crocodiles or potatoes. Unless you eat crisps in the morning, which you shouldn't.

Your journey should be short(ish) because schools are divided up into catchment areas. That means you have to live within a certain distance of the school in order to enrol there. Unless you go to a boarding school, you can't live in London and go to school in Liverpool, for example. Because of your catchment, you'll probably already know the local area, but if it's unfamiliar then maybe you can do a trial run or 'journey rehearsal'. During the summer holidays, practise getting to school from your house. Do the journey a few times so when September arrives, you'll already know your way.

Getting to school might involve bikes, buses, trains and busy streets. Some cities have free travel for under 12s or you might need a travel pass, such as an Oyster card for transport, which you can pre-load with money. Your parents or guardians can help you to apply for one in the summer holidays, as it takes a few weeks to come through. We all live in different places, so our paths to school will vary, but everyone who starts a new school may feel slightly worried on their new journey, because it's a change from what you were used to. That's natural. Everything is a bit scary when we do it for the first time, but you'll soon find your routine. All in all, secondary schools may seem like the Bermuda Triangle. They invent many new ways for you to get lost. But unlike the Bermuda Triangle, the sense of mystery doesn't last long and the fog clears quickly.

Just as there are many ways to get lost in year seven, there are also

many opportunities to find your place.

When I say find your place, I don't just mean making it to your seat in history just in time to learn about who King Henry VIII married, divorced or beheaded. I mean situating yourself in the school, being unapologetically yourself and being comfortable to express who you are in the wider community.

This is a process that requires emotional literacy. Emotional literacy isn't about reading words; it's about understanding your inner emotions and how to communicate them fluently to the outside world. In simpler terms, emotional literacy is about reading yourself, knowing how you feel and saying how you feel in your surroundings. Finding a place isn't always easy, and it doesn't happen overnight.

It's more like a gradual process of becoming more and more familiar with your new school, and the people in it, both staff and students.

So, how to find your place? At the beginning of the new term, the first thing you learn is everybody else's name. Once you've learned names, then you'll begin to work out everybody's interests and personalities. Don't panic and feel like you have to meet loads of people really quickly, and secure friends as fast as possible. It's not a race. Take your time to get to know people properly and over the first few weeks, you'll begin to make friends with kids that you previously never even knew. Yet, before long, it'll feel like you have known them for most of your life.

The best way to find your place is not to change or compromise who you are as a person – just keep being yourself and you'll be surrounded by the people most suited to you in no time. Often those will be friendships that you maintain for life.

IT'S NOT A RACE

SCHOOL RULES

There is no such thing as school without rules. You might think that would be amazing and every day would be proper fun! Trust me, it wouldn't. A school without rules would be complete chaos, and not in a good way. If you don't believe me, then read the book *Lord of the Flies* by William Golding. We actually studied it in English when we were in year seven. The whole book is about what happens when school kids live by their own rules while stranded on a desert island. I won't spoil it, but as a hint, it doesn't go well. At all.

Now, hopefully you won't be stranded on a desert island, but you can still agree that a school without rules wouldn't be a safe place where you could learn. That's the essence of rules. They are there for a reason, and that reason is to keep you safe, and to create the most suitable atmosphere for learning possible. So don't see rules as a negative, see them as something you need.

Secondary school has a lot more rules than primary. My grandad use to say, in rhyme, "Stay in line and you'll do just fine." I guess that's good advice (even though he went to school in 1918 during the First World War). You might even feel like school is a less muddy, far safer version of trench warfare, where you have to keep your head down all the time. Maybe that makes sense, but school really isn't meant to be a battleground between and your teachers.

Schools have behaviour policies. That's a written rulebook that says, "If you do this, then this will happen as a result." They are logical documents. The behaviour policy of my school back in year seven, and of most schools now, runs on a system of punishments and rewards. If we did something well, we got an *achievement point* and if we did something less than well, we got a *behaviour point*. A certain number of *achievement points* would lead to a reward, a certain number of *behaviour points* would lead to a punishment (detention). Some schools have late points if you are late, *lack of homework points* if you don't do your homework, or *lack of equipment points* if you turn up to lessons without a pen or your books. It's not too complicated really. Your school might have different names for these rewards and punishments but the thinking behind them is the same.

Behaviour points are part of school life. You'll learn about them quickly. Maybe some teachers throw out behaviour points like confetti – anyone standing near gets hit with some, guilty or not. Maybe some teachers use theirs more sparingly, like careful darts champions aiming with efficient precision. To avoid being targeted, it's really important you learn the rules of your school, so you can stay on the right side of them. If you really mess around in class you can be sent out of the classroom to wait in the corridor. This is not an ideal place to be. Usually, a teacher in the corridor, who is on call will pick you up and take you to inclusion, which is where you do work for the rest of the day in isolation. Try not to make a habit of going there.

Find out about your school policy on phones too. Some schools have a no phone policy, whereby you hand it in at the start of the day and collect it at the end. Even if your school doesn't have this rule, don't ever get caught with your phone out in lessons, that won't be allowed. Put in on silent as well, you don't want it going off in the middle of maths.

School rules increase in severity. Minor rule-breaking, like forgetting equipment, messing around a bit in class, and always being late, is met with minor punishment. In contrast, major rule breaking, such as bullying, hate speech or violence towards students or staff is met with major punishment. That makes sense though, right?

Behaviour can escalate. That means gradually get worse and worse. What starts out as fairly innocent, can slowly sour. Behaviour points can become thirty-minute detentions, which can become two-hour detentions, which can become Saturday detentions, which can become suspensions, which can become fixed-term exclusions, which can become permanent exclusions.

Don't worry though, it's not all doom and gloom. Schools want to work *with you* and not against you when it comes to behaviour, as your progress requires co-operation between you and the school;

essentially, you're a team.

Some schools will even let you have your say on the rules, this doesn't mean you're in charge, sorry, but it does mean your opinions are at least taken into account. This dialogue between staff and students generally happens in a school council. The school council is a group that meets about once a term. There are students and teachers in attendance. If you want to be on the school council, you have to be elected to represent your classmates. It's a chance to participate in politics and to improve your powers of persuasion. If you win, then you get a seat at the table, and you can present your views to the headteacher. Let's imagine for a moment that you're at the table, and the headteacher says "Okay, what are the five most important school rules in your opinion?" **What would you say?**

We tried this at the school I work at, and someone said, "My rule is no one gets in trouble for anything, ever." The headteacher said … "No." Surprise, surprise. Remember if you get into trouble, it doesn't make you a bad person. Even all the way through to permanent exclusion, that does not define you. I work with many young people who have broken school rules to the point of exclusion, and they are kids in difficult circumstances who have reacted unwisely and understandably in equal measure.

All of us react to our environment, and when things aren't going well for us, we might not behave perfectly. There is a tendency to lash out at the world, and things can get out of hand. That is understandable. Nevertheless, schools have the responsibility of creating safe learning environments. That's why actions have consequences. School rules are a tricky topic, and statistics have shown that, in the past, they were not always fairly or evenly applied on the basis of race or background. There is still a lot of progress that needs to be made to ensure equality of treatment for all when it comes to measures like permanent exclusion.

Some schools are really strict, some are less so, but either way, as you get older, you have your own responsibility to make the right choices. You are becoming an adult, and part of that is thinking for yourself. Your future, mysterious as it is, lives inside the decisions you make in the present.

So when you make your decisions, try to think, how will today impact tomorrow? Ask yourself,

am I letting myself down? Or am I making the most of my opportunities?

OPPORTUNITY COMMUNITY

Want to learn chess? I'll give the schedule
a check.
You could be a tennis ace, think of the love
you can get.
Become a netball pro or the star of
the gymnasium.
Swing a cricket bat and knock the ball out
of the stadium.

Hold a control, play a games console.
Find the football at your feet and fire
a thirty-yard goal.
Sing the chorus in the choir with
angelic harmony.
Spit bars in the rap club to Afrobeats.

Become a ballerina just to keep you on
your toes.
Shred electric guitars with energetic solos.
Direct a short film or design a magazine.
Create new worlds with a mouse and
a screen.

Get dramatic on the stage until the West
End beckons.
Win every debate, wield words
like weapons.
Sprint round the track, gold medal in your
vision.
Write poems, score slam dunks, swish,
that's the mission.

There are so many clubs, I can't wait for
you to see:
The world of opportunity community!

One of the best ways to meet people is to join a club. Whatever your interest is, there's probably a lunchtime or an after-school club for it already. If there's not – even better – because you get to make one and be the founder!

Clubs help you to form friendships and pursue your passions. Every student in your club will have a similar interest in the activity you're doing, that's why they signed up too. So it's a chance to meet like-minded people.

Clubs have a different vibe to lessons,

there is more emphasis on active collaboration and a lot less sitting in silence. You don't have to limit yourself either. There are enough clubs at secondary school for you to do something different every day of the week. It's not necessarily a club, but it's also great idea to go to the library, which provides a quiet place to catch up on homework, and an oasis of calm in contrast to the chaos of the playground – you might want that at times.

As a teacher, I run a rap club at lunchtimes and after school. It's the best. It's a way to see kids doing what they love in a space that is less restricted than the classroom. The students write and record raps and even release albums. Sometimes the kids in my rap club get double booked, because they've also signed up to read Manga comics ... do I mind? Absolutely not. The more clubs the better. Go wild!

When it comes to clubs, there is absolutely no reason that you can't be a member of chess club as well as a boxer. There is no reason you can't be both ballerina and basketballer. There is no reason you can't be a gymnast and a gamer. There is no reason to let anyone other than yourself decide what hobbies you choose. Do not waste your opportunities by caring about what is considered casually cool. Do what you want to do. That's how you make the most of the experience.

You will have the chance to go on educational trips too. Some trips might be really local to your school and involve a short bus ride to a museum. Other trips could take you further afield, you could potentially go overseas, which is really exciting. When I was in year seven we went on a football tour to France for a few days. We won every game ... success. After one match, I remember falling asleep on the minibus, and waking up with marker pen all over my face ... not success. Trips broaden your horizons and expose you to different experiences, that's how your mind grows. No one goes anywhere without a permission slip though, so make sure your parents/guardians sign on that dotted line. Because of all it offers, in the classroom and beyond it, secondary school is what I call an *opportunity community*. Which hobbies will you pick up and practise?

TESTING TIMES

One of the scariest challenges at secondary school is that dreaded word, it begins with an 'e' and ends with 's' ... can you guess? Elephants? No. Eggs? No. Exams.

Exams! I actually still hate looking at that word. No one likes exams, do they? Maybe you do; maybe you're an academic boss. Fair play. Most schools have end of year exams. That's a fact of life. The function of the exams, a bit like with SATs, is to check your learning. You need to demonstrate on paper that you haven't been daydreaming for eight months. The regularity of testing differs between schools and varies according to subject. In French we had a spelling test every Friday. In maths we had a test every couple of weeks. In other subjects, it was just once a term, or even once a year at the end.

In year seven, in most cases but not necessarily all, you will have your lessons as a form group. In teacher-speak, we call this a mixed-ability group. You are not sorted into in classes according to how well you have achieved in a certain subject. Generally, that 'sorting' occurs towards the end of year seven. Then, end-of-year exams decide which "set" you'll be placed in the following year.

To ease your worry, there are a few magic gems and jewels of knowledge for your treasure chest of exam success that I can suggest. One particular shiny piece of advice is called ... drum roll, please ... revision. I get it.

Revision is not a fun word like phantasmagoria.

(I found that word in year six actually, and it means ... nah, I'm not going to tell you what it means. You can look it up and use at school to impress your teachers!) Revision is the process of re-reading a subject, going back over it, to prepare for an examination. Revision is a gradual process that takes time, it involves regular, repeated work over a long period. Think of it like building muscle in the gym. You have to build it up slowly, bit by bit. Day by day. You can't just lift a bunch of weights non-stop in one evening and expect to be the Incredible Hulk overnight. You'll just end up strained. Similarly, you can't leave revision to a relentless, last minute frenzy. Revision doesn't need to be mind-numbingly boring though. Try to spice it up. There are different ways to revise: you can do it loudly; you can do it quietly; you can do it statue-still; you can do it on the move; you can write; you can speak; you can listen...

Revision is the type of skill that you'll need again and again. You will have revised for your SATs, so end of year exams aren't too scary because you've done all this before. Here's some pointers in the form of a rap.

REVISION RAP

Now for a rhyme, let me break down how
to revise,
And we'll do it together by counting to five.

One, you need to manage your time,
Let time be a friend that is on your side,
If you find that you're short of time,
It's very difficult to be organized.

Two, try to be organized,
No paper everywhere, just sort your life,
Maybe decorate the wall or make a folder,
And that will place less pressure on your shoulder.

Three, always get enough sleep,
A brain that is wired is tired and weak,
So, get your head down on those pillows
and sheets,
Wake up refreshed you've got levels to reach.

Four, slow down, phone down, that's the plan,
TikTok will not be in this exam,
Reels really aren't a really useful plan,
And the results aren't posted on Instagram.

Five, minds are unique with our unique lives,
We are all different in how we revise,
Find whatever works for you,
and before I end this verse for you...

Your true value is not defined by a test
For that value is the heart that's inside
of your chest.

I hope you found the rap useful. For me, the most important lines are the final two. Your true value is not defined by a test. For that value is the heart that's inside of your chest. Even though it is tempting to do it, and understandable, you should never tie your sense of self-worth to a number. Being in set one doesn't make you superior; being in set five doesn't make you inferior. There is a quote that is credited to Albert Einstein, although we are not 100% sure that he said it, which says,

> # "Everybody is a genius. But if you judge a fish by its ability to climb a tree, it will live its whole life believing that it is stupid."

This means we all have different strengths. We are naturally better at some things than others, and each of us has brilliance in our own way.

There is not just one way to be intelligent. I was good at memorizing and reproducing facts in exam conditions, but I don't think that is a truly accurate measure of intelligence. Your value is not decided by a score on a piece of paper. You are more than a piece of data on a graph. Try your best always – effort is very important – but remember you are more than a number. That is just as true in secondary school as it was in primary.

Now it's time to leave the testing times behind. We are approaching the end of part two, where we have dealt with the academic side of secondary school. The next and final part of this book is dedicated to you. It is dedicated to the personal changes and challenges that a year seven student experiences outside of the classroom, and beyond the curriculum. School is a place of learning, and not all of that learning is delivered by coffee-sipping teachers standing at the front of the classroom, or from a paragraph in a well-thumbed, worn textbook. Some of the most important learning you must do for yourself, as you grow from a child to the adult you will become. It's also what happens outside of the classroom, and beyond the school gate, that can really be the making of you.

PART 3

EXTRA-CURRICULAR

IN THE MAKING

I'm made of Rice Crispies that snap, crackle
and pop,
I'm made of 5-a-side slides, bad tackles and blocks,
Astroturf burning volcanoes into my elbows
and knees,
Felt like I was lying in lava when I was trying
to sleep.

I'm made of making my alarm clock a sworn enemy,
My deadliest nemesis from the genesis,
I vowed one day to drop kick it from my premises,
And send its shrill siren singing, through the
morning sky.

I'm made of missing shooting stars so my wishes
couldn't fly,
I'm made of being grounded if I lied,
I'm made of our house in the middle of the street,
Neighbours listening to my hip-hop beats.

Tricks not treats and sour times soothed by sweets,
I'm made of two left feet, my soul's unique,
Whatever I'm made of, I'm still in the making,
And the making is incompl—

In this poem, you've hopefully learned about a few of the things I'm made of. But this book isn't about me, it's about you, and this part of the book is specifically about what you are made of. Knowing who you are, and what is special to you is so important. In fact, so that we can start thinking about this subject, using my rhymes as inspiration, why don't you have a go at your own poem on this theme. Show me what you're made of. Find a piece of paper or a notebook, then start writing as many lines as possible with the phrase "I'm made of"...

Can you include your interests? Your passions? Your precious memories? Your dreams? What you want to be after school? Once you're ready to finish your poem, I suggest you use the line, "I'm still in the making" to close it off.

The last line is one you shouldn't forget.

You are not fully formed and set in stone. You are loading. You are in development. You are still in the making. This means there are going to be many things that change around you, including you. Don't try to fight it.

Let me put it this way, there was once a Viking king called Canute. Canute conquered most of England, and this gave him a lot of self-belief. However, he did not have so much self-belief that he thought he could control the Universe. He was a wise king, who knew that there were some things that were just bound to happen, and no one could stop them.

A story goes that he had his throne brought to the beach, where he sat upon it, and ordered the sea not to wet his ankles. Despite his proclamation, the incoming tide kept coming and coming. He ordered it not to, but the sea rose anyway, and Canute's royal feet got soaked. Then he stood up and said something like, "See what I mean, even a king can't command the waves, let alone a year six."[4]

Believing that you will never change as you grow up, is a little bit like ordering the tide not to come in.

Change is inevitable.

[4] Probably not his exact words.

In fact, like the ocean, change is beautiful. Evolution is part of life. So embrace it.

DON'T BE AFRAID TO GET YOUR FEET WET.

FRIENDSHIPS

One of the biggest fears of moving up is what will happen to your friendship group when you move schools. Although some might, not all of your friends will go to the same secondary school as you, but that doesn't mean the friendship is over. Earlier, I used the example of me and my friend Tom, who are still close friends to this day.

However, not everyone that you were friends with in primary school will continue to be your friend all the way through secondary school. That doesn't mean there is a sudden, dangerous and dramatic split, like atoms in a nuclear explosion, resulting in a huge destructive chaos. No, it's not like that. It's more like a firework slowly fizzling out. Time can bring people together, or in time, we can gradually grow apart. There are many kids from my primary who I really liked, but slowly, bit-by-bit, our paths went in separate directions. It doesn't mean we became unfriendly to each other. Growing apart is a part of growing. You will change; you will develop fresh interests and sometimes this means that friendships run their course. This is all standard.

It's distressing to think of losing old friends. It's also confusing making new ones. **Here are some quick tips.**

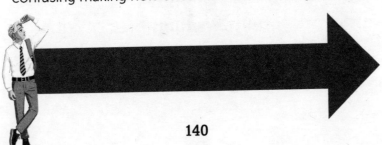

Don't rush the process, it's not about being instantly popular.

Be yourself, let people get to know the real you.

Smile and be approachable (everyone's a bit nervous, this is how you show you're friendly).

Talk to people (even if it takes you out of your comfort zone, make the first move by saying "hello" – that can go a long way).

Be co-operative in class (you'll sit next to different people in different subjects and work together, which is a great opportunity to get to know someone).

You will balance old friends and new friends, all in an unfamiliar environment with hundreds of other kids. It sounds like a lot, but you've got a lot of strength, and you'll manage just fine. Remember, if you feel jealous or confused or upset by the shifting sands of friendship, and you're not sure exactly where you stand, the best policy is always to communicate – to share how you feel. If you are struggling, remember that the struggle is temporary, and life will get better, so stay positive!

Even if you aren't argumentative, you might find yourself at some point having arguments with your friends, or having fallouts that need to be fixed – this is totally normal. When you're younger, arguments can often seem magnified.

They feel like a massive deal, a roaring flame of explosive emotions

that threaten to engulf everything.

But take a step back, keep a cool head, and you can soon extinguish that feeling. I guarantee that the problem is not as all-consuming as you thought it was at first. It's not good to act in anger, and in just a short amount of time and distance from the argument, you can think with much more clarity, which makes it far easier to solve a problem. Always try to understand someone else's point of view, to work out why they are behaving in the way they are.

Arguments are often sparked from a lack of communication, or a frustration at not being understood, so talking can help to prevent an argument. Or, after an argument, it can help to sort it out. When you talk it out, it's great to mean what you say, but not if what you are saying is mean. You can be honest without being harsh. Words are significant, they can do damage or they can heal. So we should be mindful of how we use them. Just saying one kind word can change the trajectory of someone's whole day.

ONE KIND WORD

You don't need to move a mountain,

Or rearrange the world,

All you really need is:

One kind word.

Because words can be magic,

Words can be a cure,

Words can be a bandage,

If your heart is feeling sore.

So if there's someone around you,

Maybe someone in your class,

"How are you doing today?"

That's all you need to ask.

You don't need to shout it,

You can whisper and be heard,

All you really need is one kind word.

As a year seven, just like in adulthood, there are different levels to friendship. Some friends are casual, you'll speak to each other in the playground, or play football on the same team in PE. Some friends you'll see outside of school, but maybe never talk to them deeply about your feelings. Some friends, who are your closest ones, you'll share your most honest, vulnerable emotions with. They'll help to keep you afloat if you ever find yourself in any troubled waters, and I hope you'll do the same for them.

PEER PRESSURE

When I first heard this phrase, I heard it as pier pressure. I assumed it was when friends forced each other to jump from a height into the ocean. This made sense because I grew up by the sea. In fact, my friends often pressured me to jump from stone piers that stuck out from the shore like outstretched, concrete legs. From a terrifying height, I would leap, with bent knees, closed eyes and held breath, into the swirling waves beneath, hoping I didn't land on a rock. I did it each time, so that I didn't look weak in front of my mates. That was really stupid.

In that way, pier pressure and peer pressure are exactly the same! Peer pressure is defined as:

when you are influenced by your

peers to act in a certain way.

The word "peers" is another word for "the people around you" and most often this is our friendship group, or classmates. In year seven, you will encounter peer pressure. It's like gravity – you cannot avoid it. When peer pressure gets brought up, parents and teachers often like to tell exaggerated horror stories. I'm not going to do that, but you do have to be sensible.

Peer pressure shows itself in different ways to different people, depending on the situation. Sometimes peer pressure might not require anybody saying anything at all, if someone ignores you or makes you feel like an outcast because you don't do something, that is still peer pressure. Or peer pressure can be spoken subtly enough that you might not know it's happening:

"OI, COME ON, MATE, EVERYONE'S VAPING THESE DAYS, IT'S NOT THAT DEEP, LIKE, YOU DON'T WANNA BE LEFT OUT, DO YOU, LET'S GO TO THE SHOP AND YOU CAN NICK ONE, ALL RIGHT, JUST SO YOU DON'T LIKE, STAND OUT AND SEEM WEIRD?"

Or it can be more obvious:

"IF YOU DON'T SMOKE, YEAH, EVERYONE WILL THINK YOU'RE A SCARED LITTLE LOSER."

A year seven might use a different word for loser, but that's not getting printed in this book. I referred to vaping and smoking, but peer pressure can rear its ugly head to persuade young people to do such things as to become involved with drugs or gangs, to carry knives, to skip school, to shoplift or commit crime. You name it, peer pressure will be involved to some degree. These examples are serious, but they are not common, so don't worry. It is unlikely that you will be faced with those scenarios – but it is good to be aware.

LET'S PLAY TRUE OR FALSE...

1. If you don't do what someone says you will lose your friendship with them.

2. Peer pressure can only come from your friends.

3. Bad behaviour is okay if you were doing it because of peer pressure.

All these statements are false. I'm sorry, I tricked you. The truth is that peer pressure comes from wanting to fit in, but retaining your individuality doesn't mean you will lose friends. Peer pressure does not just come from your friendship group, it can also come from family members, from the media or online. Peer pressure is also no excuse for bad behaviour, it does not mean you have no individual responsibility for your actions.

In the 1980s, long before you were born, there was a Hollywood actor who become President of the USA. His name was Ronald Reagan. Reagan's wife, the First Lady, Nancy Reagan, started a famous campaign against peer pressure, specifically in relation to taking drugs. She used three words to sum up her message: Just Say No. But this messaging, though it had good intentions, was way too simple. Life is more complex. What Nancy Reagan didn't realize was how powerful peer pressure can be. We don't all have the same backgrounds, and in some places, safety and success are harder to reach than others. When you don't feel safe, it's more difficult to make the right choices. That's when peer pressure becomes even more forceful and has a more dangerous effect. It's never as simple as just saying no – it can be very hard to say no –

and it takes a lot of courage to do so.

In year seven, I'm not sure that I had that kind of courage. It was something that I developed later on in my school life.

So what do you do? I am not going to tell you to Just Say No. Well, I sort of am, but not in those words. I don't want to preach to you. I am not your parent, and for most of you reading this, I am not your teacher. But I can give you some advice if you'll let me.

Always remember who you are as a person and maintain that emotional literacy that has given you an understanding of yourself.

Know what you are comfortable with and know what

makes you uncomfortable.

Know what actions you would be proud of, and what actions would mean you have let yourself down. Sometimes, in trying to appear cool in year seven, I lost a sense of my own identity, and that's a terrible thing to lose. If being "cool" is what you want to be, trust me, there's nothing "cooler" than an individual who is unafraid to be who they are, who doesn't bow down to pressure from anyone, who knows what's right, what's wrong and who knows their own mind. That is the sort of young person that you should try to be. Deal?

BULLYING

This section is going to sound serious. But don't be alarmed. There is no need to worry. I'm going to talk about bullying, so you can have all the information you need to prevent it or report it – but that doesn't mean that you will experience it. It's good to be informed though.

How do we define bullying? According to the Anti-Bullying Alliance in the UK, bullying is the "repetitive, intentional hurting of one person or group by another person or group, where the relationship involves an imbalance of power. Bullying can be physical, verbal or psychological. It can happen face-to-face or online".

Bullying is repetitive and intentional, that means is carried out again and again, deliberately and knowingly. Further unpicking this definition, let's clarify what is meant by an imbalance of power. This refers to when a young person, or a group of young people feel like they have power over somebody else. This perception of power might be a matter of numbers, where someone is in the majority group and picks on a minority group. Power might come from physical strength, from 'higher' social standing, having more money, or from simply being older than a victim. The reasons behind this behaviour can be complex.

Nowadays, the traditional view that bullying just involves a 'bully' and a 'victim' has been shown as somewhat inaccurate. The picture is more complicated. From the research undertaken by the Anti-Bullying Alliance, what we know now is that bullying rarely takes place between a 'bully' and a 'victim' alone. Bullying is more likely to stem from group behaviour, involving a number of people in a series of roles.

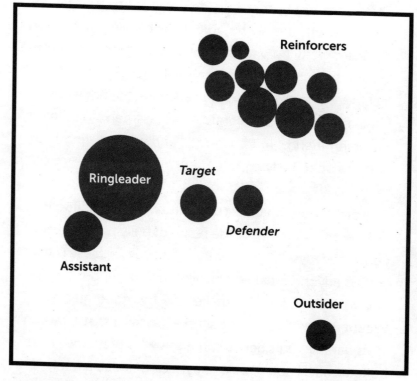

Bullying often involves a 'ringleader' who carries out the majority of bullying on a 'target', whilst encouraging others to join in. There is also a group that can be called 'reinforcers' who give power to the 'ringleader'. This group might not be directly involved, but will laugh at what the ringleader does, gather people to see what's happening, or encourage the bullying activity. If someone directly joins in with the bullying, although they didn't start it, they can be referred to as an 'assistant' because they help out the 'ringleaders'.

On the other side, there are 'defenders' – this is a person or group who helps the 'target' of bullying. They may do this directly by physically or verbally confronting the 'ringleader' or in a less direct way, by telling a teacher. A 'defender' might question or undermine the power of the ringleader in front of 'reinforcers' or 'assistants', as well as providing friendship to a 'target' and empowering them to stand up to bullying.

One of the worst and most shameful ways I was influenced by peer pressure, was in the realm of bullying. For years, I convinced myself that I was the good guy, because I never bullied anyone. I did see bullying going on, but I would never be involved. That makes me the good guy, right? Except, it's not really that simple. I realize that I was an 'outsider'. An 'outsider' is someone who pretends not to notice what is going on, or stays out of it deliberately.

If there's bullying going on around you, but you don't join in, you might think you are doing enough of the right things. Wrong.

IT IS NOT ENOUGH TO DO OR SAY NOTHING.

If you are not actively speaking out, calling out the bullying or telling a teacher, then you are part of the problem. Rather than solely focusing on changing the behaviour of a 'ringleader' – we should focus on changing the behaviour of a whole group. Everybody has a part to play.

So much of my work as a teacher revolves around anti-bullying. I'm glad the message is getting out there, one of my raps, which has millions of views and has appeared on *BBC Newsround*, is all about the subject. Here it is – rap along if you want!

TAKE THAT TIME TO TALK TO THE TEAM

When somebody is acting mean,

Take that time to talk to the team.

Somebody posted unkind memes,

Take that time to talk to the team.

Somebody stole my brand-new jeans,

Take that time to talk to the team.

Unkind words impact my dreams,

Take that time to talk to the team.

I ain't got time for bullies,

I see that and I hate that fully,

Not big, not smart nor clever, no excuse for that,

not ever.

Sticks and stones can break your bones,

Words can hurt you sent on phones,

If you need help, you're not alone,

Tell somebody at school or home.

Most bullies are victims too,

They feel hurt so they do it to you.

Like I said, that's no excuse,

We've all got things that we're going through.

Remember the verse, just like I thought it,

Chat bad then you get reported.

Remember the word, just like I taught it,

See it, say it, sorted!

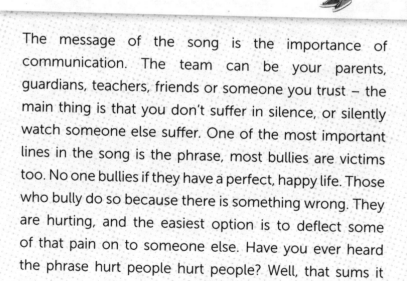

The message of the song is the importance of communication. The team can be your parents, guardians, teachers, friends or someone you trust – the main thing is that you don't suffer in silence, or silently watch someone else suffer. One of the most important lines in the song is the phrase, most bullies are victims too. No one bullies if they have a perfect, happy life. Those who bully do so because there is something wrong. They are hurting, and the easiest option is to deflect some of that pain on to someone else. Have you ever heard the phrase hurt people hurt people? Well, that sums it up. Does that make it okay? No. My mum used to say,

"Christian, imagine you are wearing a cloak of mirrors." The meaning behind this was that other people's words are really a reflection of them, and not you. If someone is unkind, then that unkindness is on them, not you at all. Keep your head up and take that time to talk to the team. Like peer pressure, bullying comes in many forms. If we were to sort it into categories then there are three main types of bullying.

PHYSICAL BULLYING

Physical bullying involves violence. This can be pushing, shoving, punching, biting, touching, grabbing ... this kind of thing. It is the easiest sign of bullying to spot, and because of that, it is perhaps the least seen in schools. It is not as common as other forms of bullying, but always be on the lookout.

EMOTIONAL OR VERBAL BULLYING

This was the bullying that I saw in year seven. It consists of name-calling, ridiculing, humiliating, excluding, spreading lies or rumours, making threats, insults and emotional abuse. Emotional bullying causes harm without physical violence, but that doesn't make it any less serious. Emotional bullying is harder to detect than physical bullying, it does not leave a visible scar or bruise, yet it causes much mental distress. It's really important to take that time to talk to the team if you experience or witness it.

CYBERBULLYING

Cyberbullying is defined as an aggressive, intentional act, carried out by a group or individual, using electronic forms of contact. This occurs repeatedly and over time, against a target who cannot easily defend themselves.

This was barely a thing when I was at school. Cyberbullying was only just emerging as we were gaining access to the internet. But you could only use the internet if your parents weren't on the phone. It took about five minutes to dial up. Now, the world is different. Cyberbullying is currently a very widespread form of bullying. In 2020, according to statistics from Cybercrew, one in five children in the UK, aged between ten and fifteen experienced cyberbullying.

Cyberbullying is often the hardest form of bullying for adults to detect, it can occur 24/7 and most of it happens outside of school. Cyberbullying can consist of unwanted messages, pictures, videos and is most often found on social media or gaming platforms. Because teachers might not know about cyberbullying, it is really important that you tell them, or someone at home, otherwise it can't be addressed. Take that time to the talk to the team. Let's keep saying that until it sticks!

As well as online, bullying does not just happen in one place, it can occur in corridors and hallways between lessons, in the classroom, in the canteen, on the school bus, in the bathrooms and changing rooms or outside of school. Just like my rap said, whenever, wherever you see it, you need to say it, so it can get sorted.

Okay, we made it. I know that this chapter was tough going, but I don't want it to scare you, just inform you. The likelihood is that everything is going to be completely fine, but we also have to be real, and acknowledge that bullying exists. But now that you know what to look out for, and what to do, you can help to stop bullying and help create a better, safer, school environment for everyone.

(ANTI-)SOCIAL MEDIA

Social media is defined as websites, apps and games that connect people to each other, through pictures, videos, information, ideas, messages and other content. Social media can be accessed through smart phones or via computers. It seems to be absolutely everywhere these days, but it wasn't always this way. Social media is less than twenty years old. In 2004, when I was in year seven, the first social medium to reach one million users was called MySpace. I bet you've never heard of it. It doesn't exist anymore. Today in 2023,

YouTube has 2.7 billion users (that's a significant proportion of the planet).

WhatsApp has 2 billion users. TikTok has 1.5 billion users and Instagram has 1.35 billion users. That's a lot of online content.

All of this stuff on cyberspace generates a wide range of opinions. As with any technology, there are positives and negatives that are attached to social media.

POSITIVES

Social media can connect communities who share similar interests, from makeup to Roblox to the Roman Empire – there's a group for you.

Social media permits you to express yourself freely, to share your opinions and perspective of the world with other people.

Social media is a free source of information that contains educational materials.

Social media supports and encourages creativity, whether you're a surfer or a streamer, it helps you to showcase your skills.

NEGATIVES

Social media is deliberately addictive. It is also proven to be damaging to mental health. Its use is linked to increased anxiety, poorer sleep patterns and higher rates of depression.

Although you can access news on social media, this news is not always verified and can be fake. There are huge amounts of misinformation online, which can be used to influence your way of thinking.

Social media can be a forum for online bullying, through hateful content and trolling.

Social media can promote unrealistic beauty standards, which leads to issues with body image and lower self-esteem.

Can you think of any other pros and cons for social media? Social media platforms have a minimum age limit to sign up to them, which is thirteen years old. We need to be honest though, many year sixes and sevens use social media already, despite this limit – so it's really important to discuss it.

As Peter Parker's Uncle Ben says in Spiderman, "With great power comes great responsibility." Social media gives you an immense level of power to take your unfiltered thoughts and post them straight to the world in a millisecond. However, with this power, comes the responsibility to be very, very careful.

When you post something online, even if you delete it, it might stay there forever.

So do not post without thinking of the future. Do you want your post to stay online for all eternity?

Social media is not real life. It's as simple as that. I now it on a personal level. Even though I'm a different generation, I'm on TikTok, I've got an Instagram, all of that stuff. On my social media channels, there are over thirty million views and hundreds of thousands of followers. The Christian Foley that they see on screen is, in many ways, a completely different Christian Foley to the person writing this book. To tell you the truth, that number of views makes me feel uncomfortable. I am not fooled into thinking I am anything special, just because people click on my page. From a "follower" point of view, I am a successful rapper and teacher, whose lessons never go wrong, who has the perfect career, who smiles all the time and breezes through life. Sorry to disappoint you, but that's just not true. Sure, it looks that way, because I only show you what I want you to see, but social media is a mask. It's a disguise, a flashy form of false advertising.

In reality, I have failed many more times than I have succeeded. I just didn't post it online. In real life, every lesson does not go to plan, every rap I write is not a smash hit, and I am not always smiling. Sometimes, like many teachers, I feel exhausted, stressed out and anxious about the progress of myself and my class. That's completely normal. So when you see someone on Instagram, TikTok or Snapchat who has a so-called perfect existence, remember, to some extent, it's just a performance. I'll say it again, social media is not real life. However, social media can significantly impact real life. What you do on there has consequences for your own non-virtual life, and for other people's. So be responsible with what you produce.

Also, be mindful of what you consume. Do not worry about what you eat and what you wear, what you look like and what you think is down to you. Be careful of influencers who tell you how to exist. What are their qualifications? When you log on to social media, you are bombarded with more information than you can process; it's too much to digest, overwhelming.

Scroll. Scroll. Scroll. It's addictive.

With each flick of the forefinger, there's another video served up by the algorithm. In the face of all this stimulation, information and misinformation, you need to have a critical mind. This means you need to be able to make your own decisions, to think for yourself and not just blindly accept what you are told, because it comes from someone who calls themselves a "Top G" and apparently has a garage stacked with Lamborghinis. You need to be able to separate what is real, and what is not. Do not be too influenced by influencers. When you can do that, then you can blunt the sharp danger of social media and start to appreciate its benefits. It's not all doom and gloom.

As we previously spoke about, social media also has positives. For starters, the dog videos are awesome, or, if you're a cat person, the cat videos are awesome. There are TikTok accounts that recommend books: that's awesome. There are education channels (like mine, I guess) that help you to learn. There are nature channels that show you exactly how a grizzly bear catches salmon. There are so many opportunities to access knowledge through social media when it is used responsibly, with a critical mind. Social media gives us a chance to connect with one another instantly.

Recently, Safer Internet Day, a UK charity who, as their name suggests, work towards establishing a safer internet for children, asked me to write a poem about the connections that the internet and social media provides. I think it will be useful for you to see an extract of it.

CONNECTIONS

Fishing for likes and trawling through trolls,
Scrawling more comments, we scroll and we scroll,
But why should we subscribe to YouTube haters,
Or base our status on notifications?

Instagram grapples, we wrestle with self-image,
TikTok, we clock up our hours unfinished,
Watching the feed, fed up with the 'For You Page',
Because we're still not full, we keep scrolling for days,
To the rhythm of the algorithm, we dance, we vibe,
But remember it's more important to live, than to
"go live".

These days we don't chat, we Snapchat,
But it's time to snap back to reality,
Before we lose ourselves to what's trending…
The future is not a GPS with pre-mapped directions,
And Siri's serious suggestions or lectures from Alexa,
So go outside, interact in real life, there's
no question…
You don't need Wi-Fi or 5G network detection,
To make meaningful and long-lasting,
actual connections.

RELATIONSHIPS

Both online and offline, secondary schools are places where a whole lot of gossip seems to swirl around. There's a lot of,

"He said, she said, they said."

Everyone knows everyone else's business, or at least they think they do. I guess gossip has always been part of the human experience. There were probably cavemen talking behind each other's backs.

The definition of gossip is *to talk about other people's business, typically involving details that aren't confirmed as true*. People might like to gossip, but the thing is, no one likes to be the subject of gossip. So, if you're sitting round the canteen eating a lovely school dinner (mine used to be jacket potato) and everyone is talking about someone, just have a think. Spreading rumours can be hurtful, even if you don't think you're doing anything wrong. Think, *would I want everyone talking about me in this way? Are we speaking negatively about someone, and is that right?* Gossip isn't always negative. It can be neutral or positive as well. For example you could say nice things about someone when they're not there – there's nothing wrong with that at all! But when it comes to gossip, I'll quote my mum again, who always uses the classic mum-like phrase,

"If you haven't got anything nice to say, don't say anything at all."

That's good advice to be honest.

One of the main areas of gossip tends to be about relationships. Who fancies who? You could probably have a school radio station on the subject that broadcasts uninterrupted 24/7 with live phone-ins and interviews.

In year seven, you are suddenly thrown together with hundreds of new people, and it's natural as you're getting older that you might fancy a few of them.

Young love is a minefield. One wrong move and it feels like your whole world blows up. Because you haven't had romantic relationships before, everything feels intense, from the adrenaline that rushes through your body when you like someone, to the wrenching pain in your chest when it doesn't work out. Before thinking about other people, have a think – what is your relationship with your own mind like? Do you forgive yourself for mistakes? Are you too hard on yourself? We can sometimes be our own harshest critics. But having a healthy relationship with yourself is crucial when thinking of establishing relationships with others.

Don't lose sight of your own self-worth.

Often we find it easier to identify our weaknesses, than we do to say positive things about ourselves.

Maybe we need to practise more.

Let's do it. Go on, on a piece of paper or in a notebook, write five things that you like about yourself.

That wasn't too painful was it? As well as a sense of self-worth, knowing your own values and principles is also vital, because then you can judge whether they are compatible with someone else's. Most books and movies like to sell the story of a soulmate and say that there is just one person in the Universe for you. This might make you feel pressure to find a soulmate at school. Where are they?

Beside the vending machines? In the canteen? By lost property?

I might sound a bit cynical here, but if I'm being real, then real life isn't Disney, so please don't burden yourself with too many unrealistic expectations of fairy-tale romances that last from year seven until forever. I'm not saying it doesn't happen, ever. Anything is possible. But I'm saying that you shouldn't expect it to be like the movies and put yourselves under extra stress.

Relationships aren't straightforward, they can be healthy or unhealthy, or a mix of both. Before entering into a relationship, or 'catching feelings', it's useful to be able to recognize the difference between what is healthy, and what is not.

SPENDING TIME TOGETHER = HEALTHY

It's good to spend time together, and to do things that you enjoy, which strengthens your bond. If you both like the cinema, why not load up on pick 'n' mix and have a sweet time?

SPENDING ALL YOUR TIME TOGETHER = UNHEALTHY

It's not good to spend all of your available time together, no matter how strong your feelings are, you don't need to stick together every second of every hour of every day. Everyone needs a break from someone else now and then. A relationship should never limit how often you interact with your friends and family, nor should anyone make you feel guilty for spending time with other people – that's controlling behaviour.

BEING OPEN AND HONEST = HEALTHY

It is good to have honest communication between one another. You should feel safe to express your emotions, positive or negative, without fear of judgement or ridicule. Being able to say "today I'm anxious, or I'm feeling sad or scared about something" is all part of a healthy relationship.

BEING BRUTALLY HONEST AND CRITICAL = UNHEALTHY

It's not good to be so honest that it verges on disrespect. Being brutally honest can damage someone's self-esteem. If you are asked, "How do I look in this outfit?" and you say, "I'm just being honest, you look terrible, I'd be embarrassed to walk down the street with you." That's just bordering on offensive, to be honest.

NEVER ARGUING = HEALTHY/UNHEALTHY

If you get on so well that an argument is a rarity, that's great and sounds like a good, healthy thing. But it might also mean that you are afraid to fully express yourself, for fear of what might happen. Relationships involve dialogue and co-operation and it is natural to have disagreements, which can be resolved by talking things through maturely.

ARGUING ALL THE TIME = UNHEALTHY

Yes, it's natural to have occasional disagreements. But not all the time. If you are constantly arguing, either in person or over text, typing back and forth, always watching the screen, waiting for a message, this is unhealthy.

Being able to identify the healthy and unhealthy aspects of relationships, will help you to look after yourself and your friends as you navigate this emotional maze. This is an awkward time in your lives. Everything is changing around you, and you and your body are changing too. As you go through puberty, your hormones kick in and that's a bit of a rollercoaster. Look, I'm not going to sit here and give you dating advice.

I went on one date in year seven, to the cinema, we went to watch *The Incredibles* and it was incredibly disastrous!

All I can say is, no one owes you their time, attention and affection, and you don't owe it to anyone else either. You don't have a certified right to anyone else, and they don't have a right to you. Relationships should never involve controlling behaviour, peer pressure or coercion. Don't be pressured into asking anyone out if you don't want to, or saying yes to anything you don't want to do. If you ask someone out and they're not into it, don't endlessly keep trying – that's not a good look. Like that famous old song says, it's about R-E-S-P-E-C-T. Respect yourself and your boundaries, and the boundaries of other people. You're all in this together.

MOVING UP

What do you say when you leave year six?

So many subjects in the mix,

Original problems you gotta fix,

You say, "We're moving up."

Got more mates in your friendship group,

Some friends old and some friends new,

Routines switch up from outta the blue,

Expect it, moving up.

You get lost then you find your way,

Relationships to navigate,

Childhood changed when you passed

those gates,

That's part of moving up.

Exams, detentions, stricter rules,

But way more clubs you can join

at school,

This is your time to shine, you jewels,

Enjoy it, moving up.

The real world fuses with

internet illusions,

Questions, queries, and quiet confusions,

But all those problems have solutions,

They're all in this book.

SUMMING UP

H ere you are at the end of the book. It feels like quite the journey. If you had those nagging pinches of nerves about secondary school, I hope they've been soothed. If you were a fizzing firework of excitement, I hope you're even more enthusiastic than you were. If you just needed to know what to expect, I hope you're now well-informed, well-equipped and ready to go.

Once at secondary school, you'll realize that the process of "Moving Up" isn't really too complicated. At a basic level, it involves that old saying, some things change, some things stay the same. The saying also applies to you. In some ways you will change, and in some ways, you will be the person that you have always been. Whoever you are, wherever you're reading this, know that

you are as unique as your fingerprint, and you will

leave a mark on this world in your own individual way.

Secondary school is the next stage of your progression. Remember, it's going to be unforgettable. So go out there and make your memories. These moments will shape you, just as they shaped me. You've got this!

During the writing of this book, I went back to my old secondary school to speak to the new year sevens, who sat in the same assembly hall that I used to. The same hall where the headteacher gave us the welcome speech and told us how smart our blazers looked. The current headteacher asked me to inspire the year sevens, to give them words of encouragement on their journey through secondary school. I knew what to say to them and I'll say it to you. **You deserve your shoutouts.**

SHOUTOUT TO YEAR SEVENS

Shoutout to year sevens,

Unphased, always on point like lasers,

Smart with witty remarks, tongues sharp as razors,

Tastemakers, styled out in your brand-new blazers.

Shout out to year sevens,

The world is a basketball in your grip,

As you bounce from subject to subject,

Ballet dance with undone laces and still don't trip.

Shout out to year sevens,

The next generation, fly like levitation,

Pledging dedication to your education,

Chasing the edge of the ledge of greatness,

Take your place … there's room enough,

You'll make it through when school gets tough,

That's all for now, I wish you good luck.

Shout out to year sevens … keep **MOVING UP!**

INDEX